let's cook

chicken

Tom
Bridge

p

Contents

Cream of Chicken Soup

Tarragon adds a delicate aniseed flavour to this tasty soup.
If you can't find tarragon, use parsley for a fresh taste.

Serves 4

INGREDIENTS

60 g/2 oz/4 tbsp unsalted butter
1 large onion, peeled and chopped
300 g/10$\frac{1}{2}$ oz cooked chicken,
  shredded finely
600 ml/1 pint/2$\frac{1}{2}$ cups chicken stock
1 tbsp chopped fresh tarragon

150 ml/$\frac{1}{4}$ pint/$\frac{2}{3}$ cup double
  (heavy) cream
salt and pepper
fresh tarragon leaves, to garnish
deep fried croûtons, to serve

1 Melt the butter in a large saucepan and fry the onion for 3 minutes.

2 Add the chicken to the pan with 300 ml/$\frac{1}{2}$ pint/1$\frac{1}{4}$ cups of the chicken stock.

3 Bring to the boil and simmer for 20 minutes. Allow to cool, then liquidize the soup.

4 Add the remainder of the stock and season with salt and pepper.

5 Add the chopped tarragon, pour the soup into a tureen or individual serving bowls and add a swirl of cream.

6 Garnish the soup with fresh tarragon and serve with deep fried croûtons.

VARIATION

To make garlic croûtons, crush 3–4 garlic cloves in a pestle and mortar and add to the oil.

VARIATION

If you can't find fresh tarragon, freeze-dried tarragon makes a good substitute. Single (light) cream can be used instead of the double (heavy) cream.

Coronation Chicken

This classic salad is good as a starter or as part of a buffet.
Mango chutney makes a tasty addition.

Serves 6

INGREDIENTS

4 tbsp olive oil
900 g/2 lb chicken meat, diced
125 g/4^1/2 oz/^{2}/3 cup rindless,
   smoked bacon, diced
12 shallots
2 garlic cloves, crushed

1 tbsp mild curry powder
300 ml/^{1}/2 pint/1^1/4 cups mayonnaise
1 tbsp runny honey
1 tbsp chopped fresh parsley
90 g/3 oz/^{1}/2 cup seedless black
   grapes, quartered

pepper
cold saffron rice, to serve

1 Heat the oil in a large frying pan (skillet) and add the chicken, bacon, shallots, garlic and curry powder. Cook slowly for about 15 minutes.

2 Spoon the mixture into a clean mixing bowl.

3 Allow the mixture to cool completely then season with pepper to taste.

4 Blend the mayonnaise with a little honey, then add the chopped fresh parsley. Toss the chicken in the mixture.

5 Place the mixture in a deep serving dish, garnish with the grapes and serve with cold saffron rice.

COOK'S TIP

You can use this recipe to fill a jacket potato or as a sandwich filling, but cut the chicken into smaller pieces.

VARIATION

Add 2 tbsp chopped fresh apricots and 2 tbsp flaked (slivered) almonds to the sauce in step 4. For a healthier version of this dish, replace the mayonnaise with the same quantity of natural (unsweetened) yogurt and omit the honey otherwise the sauce will be too runny.

Poached Breast of Chicken with Whisky Sauce

After cooking with stock and vegetables, chicken breasts are served with a velvety sauce made from whisky and crème fraîche.

Serves 6

INGREDIENTS

25 g/1 oz/2 tbsp butter
60 g/2 oz/^{1}/2 cup shredded leeks
60 g/2 oz/^{1}/3 cup diced carrot
60 g/2 oz/^{1}/4 cup diced celery
4 shallots, sliced

600 ml/1 pint/2^1/2 cups chicken stock
6 chicken breasts
50 ml/2 fl oz/^{1}/4 cup whisky
200 ml/7 fl oz/1 scant cup crème fraîche

2 tbsp freshly grated horseradish
1 tsp honey, warmed
1 tsp chopped fresh parsley
salt and pepper
sprig of fresh parsley, to garnish

1 Melt the butter in a large saucepan and add the leeks, carrot, celery and shallots. Cook for 3 minutes, add half the chicken stock and cook for about 8 minutes.

2 Add the remaining chicken stock, bring to the boil, add the chicken breasts and cook for 10 minutes.

3 Remove the chicken and thinly slice. Place on a large, hot serving dish and keep warm until required.

4 In another saucepan, heat the whisky until reduced by half. Strain the chicken stock through a fine sieve, add to the pan and reduce the liquid by half.

5 Add the crème fraîche, the horseradish and the honey. Heat gently and add the chopped parsley and salt and pepper to taste. Stir until well blended.

6 Pour a little of the whisky sauce around the chicken and pour the remaining sauce into a sauceboat to serve.

7 Serve with a vegetable patty made from the leftover vegetables, mashed potato and fresh vegetables. Garnish with the parsley sprig.

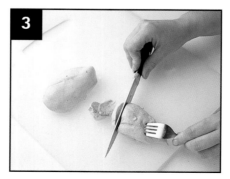

Golden Glazed Chicken

A glossy glaze with sweet and fruity flavours coats chicken breasts in this tasty recipe.

Serves 6

INGREDIENTS

6 boneless chicken breasts
1 tsp turmeric
1 tbsp wholegrain
   (whole-grain) mustard
300 ml/^{1}/$_2$ pint/1^1/$_4$ cups
   orange juice

2 tbsp clear honey
2 tbsp sunflower oil
350 g/12 oz/1^1/$_2$ cups
   long grain rice
1 orange
3 tbsp chopped mint

salt and pepper
mint sprigs, to garnish

1 With a sharp knife, mark the surface of the chicken breasts in a diamond pattern. Mix together the turmeric, mustard, orange juice and honey and pour over the chicken. Chill until required.

2 Lift the chicken from the marinade and pat dry on paper towels.

3 Heat the oil in a wide pan, add the chicken and sauté until golden, turning once. Drain off any excess oil. Pour over the marinade, cover and simmer for 10–15 minutes until the chicken is tender.

4 Boil the rice in lightly salted water until tender and drain well. Finely grate the rind from the orange and stir into the rice with the mint.

5 Using a sharp knife, remove the peel and white pith from the orange and cut the flesh into segments.

6 Serve the chicken with the orange and mint rice, garnished with orange segments and mint sprigs.

VARIATION

To make a slightly sharper sauce, use small grapefruit instead of the oranges.

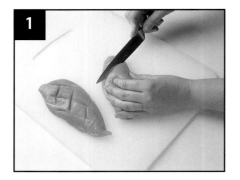

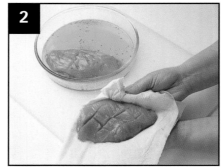

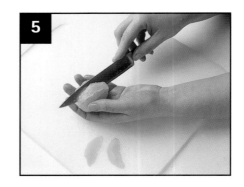

Mediterranean Chicken Parcels

This method of cooking makes the chicken aromatic and succulent. It also reduces the amount of oil needed since the chicken and vegetables cook in their own juices.

Serves 6

INGREDIENTS

1 tbsp olive oil
6 skinless chicken breast fillets
250 g/9 oz/2 cups Mozzarella
  cheese

500 g/1 lb 2 oz/3^{1}/$_2$ cups courgettes
  (zucchini), sliced
6 large tomatoes, sliced
1 small bunch fresh basil or oregano

pepper
rice or pasta, to serve

1 Cut six pieces of foil each about 25cm/10 inches square. Brush the foil squares lightly with oil and set aside until required.

2 With a sharp knife, slash each chicken breast at intervals, then slice the Mozzarella cheese and place between the cuts in the chicken.

3 Divide the courgettes (zucchini) and tomatoes between the pieces of foil and sprinkle with black pepper. Tear or roughly chop the basil or oregano and scatter over the vegetables in each parcel.

4 Place the chicken on top of each pile of vegetables then wrap in the foil to enclose the chicken and vegetables, tucking in the ends.

5 Place on a baking tray (cookie sheet) and bake in a preheated oven, 200°C/400°C/Gas Mark 6, for about 30 minutes.

6 To serve, unwrap each foil parcel and serve with rice or pasta.

COOK'S TIP

To aid cooking, place the vegetables and chicken on the shiny side of the foil so that once the parcel is wrapped up the dull surface of the foil is facing outwards. This ensures that the heat is absorbed into the parcel and not reflected away from it.

Golden Chicken Risotto

If you prefer, ordinary long grain rice can be used instead of risotto rice, but it won't give you the traditional, deliciously creamy texture that is typical of Italian risottos.

Serves 4

INGREDIENTS

2 tbsp sunflower oil
15 g/^{1}/$_2$ oz/1 tbsp butter
   or margarine
1 medium leek, thinly sliced
1 large yellow (bell) pepper, diced
3 skinless, boneless chicken breasts,
   diced
350 g/12 oz round grain
   (arborio) rice

few strands saffron
1.5 litres/2^3/$_4$ pints/6^1/$_4$ cups chicken
   stock
200 g/7 oz can sweetcorn
   (corn-on-the-cob)
60 g/2 oz/^{1}/$_2$ cup toasted
   unsalted peanuts

60 g/2 oz/^{1}/$_2$ cup grated
   Parmesan cheese
salt and pepper

1 Heat the oil and butter or margarine in a large saucepan. Fry the leek and (bell) pepper for 1 minute then stir in the chicken and cook, stirring until golden brown.

2 Stir in the rice and cook for 2–3 minutes.

3 Stir in the saffron strands, and salt and pepper to taste.

Add the stock, a little at a time, cover and cook over a low heat, stirring occasionally, for about 20 minutes, until the rice is tender and most of the liquid is absorbed. Do not let the risotto dry out – add more stock if necessary.

4 Stir in the sweetcorn (corn-on-the-cob), peanuts and Parmesan cheese, then adjust the seasoning to taste. Serve hot.

COOK'S TIP

Risottos can be frozen, before adding the Parmesan cheese, for up to 1 month, but remember to reheat this risotto thoroughly as it contains chicken.

Spiced Chicken Casserole

Spices, herbs, fruit, nuts and vegetables are combined to make an appealing casserole with lots of flavour.

Serves 4–6

INGREDIENTS

3 tbsp olive oil
900 g/2 lb chicken meat, sliced
10 shallots or pickling onions
3 carrots, chopped
60 g/2 oz/^{1}/$_2$ cup chestnuts, sliced
60 g/2 oz/^{1}/$_2$ cup flaked (slivered)
  almonds, toasted
1 tsp freshly grated nutmeg
3 tsp ground cinnamon

300 ml/^{1}/$_2$ pint/1^1/$_4$ cups white wine
300 ml/^{1}/$_2$ pint/1^1/$_4$ cups chicken
  stock
175 ml/6 fl oz/^{3}/$_4$ cup white wine
  vinegar
1 tbsp chopped fresh tarragon
1 tbsp chopped fresh flat leaf parsley
1 tbsp chopped fresh thyme
grated rind of 1 orange

1 tbsp dark muscovado sugar
125 g/4^1/$_2$ oz/^{3}/$_4$ cup
  seedless black grapes, halved
sea salt and pepper
fresh herbs, to garnish
wild rice or puréed potato, to serve

---

1 Heat the olive oil in a large saucepan and fry the chicken, shallots or pickling onions, and carrots for about 6 minutes or until browned.

2 Add the remaining ingredients, except the grapes, and simmer over a low heat for 2 hours until the meat is very tender. Stir the casserole occasionally.

3 Add the grapes just before serving and serve with wild rice or puréed potato. Garnish with herbs.

VARIATION

Experiment with different types of nuts and fruits – try sunflower seeds instead of the almonds, and add 2 fresh apricots, chopped.

COOK'S TIP

This casserole would also be delicious served with thick slices of crusty wholemeal (whole wheat) bread to soak up the sauce.

Fricassée of Chicken in Lime Sauce

The addition of lime juice and lime rind adds a delicious tangy flavour to this chicken stew.

Serves 4

INGREDIENTS

1 large chicken, cut into small portions
60 g/2 oz/$\frac{1}{2}$ cup flour, seasoned
2 tbsp oil
500 g/1 lb 2 oz baby onions or shallots, sliced

1 each green and red (bell) pepper, sliced thinly
150 ml/$\frac{1}{4}$ pint/$\frac{2}{3}$ cup chicken stock
juice and rind of 2 limes
2 chillies, chopped
2 tbsp oyster sauce

1 tsp Worcestershire sauce
salt and pepper

1 Coat the chicken pieces in the seasoned flour. Heat the oil in a large frying pan (skillet) and cook the chicken for about 4 minutes until browned all over.

2 Using a slotted spoon, transfer the chicken to a large, deep casserole and sprinkle with the sliced onions. Keep warm until required.

3 Slowly fry the (bell) peppers in the juices remaining in the frying pan (skillet).

4 Add the chicken stock, lime juice and rind and cook for a further 5 minutes.

5 Add the chillies, oyster sauce and Worcestershire sauce. Season with salt and pepper to taste.

6 Pour the (bell) peppers and juices over the chicken and onions.

7 Cover the casserole with a lid or cooking foil.

8 Cook in the centre of a preheated oven, 190°C/375°F/Gas Mark 5, for 1$\frac{1}{2}$ hours until the chicken is very tender, then serve.

COOK'S TIP

Try this casserole with a cheese scone (biscuit) topping. About 30 minutes before the end of cooking time, simply top with rounds cut from cheese scone (biscuit) pastry.

Country Chicken Bake

This economical bake is a complete meal – its crusty, herb-flavoured French bread topping mops up the tasty juices, and means there's no need to serve potatoes or rice separately.

Serves 4

INGREDIENTS

2 tbsp sunflower oil
4 chicken quarters
16 small whole onions, peeled
3 sticks (stalks) celery, sliced
400 g/14 oz can red kidney beans
4 medium tomatoes, quartered

200 ml/7 fl oz/ scant 1 cup
   dry cider or stock
4 tbsp chopped fresh parsley
1 tsp paprika
60 g/2 oz/4 tbsp butter
12 slices French bread

salt and pepper

---

1 Heat the oil in a flameproof casserole and fry the chicken quarters two at a time until golden. Using a slotted spoon, remove the chicken from the pan and set aside until required.

2 Add the onions and fry, turning occasionally, until golden brown. Add the celery and fry for 2–3 minutes. Return the chicken to the pan, then stir in the beans, tomatoes, cider, half the parsley, salt and pepper. Sprinkle with the paprika.

3 Cover and cook in a preheated oven, 200°C/400°F/ Gas Mark 6, for 20–25 minutes, until the chicken juices run clear when pierced with a skewer.

4 Mix the remaining parsley with the butter and spread evenly over the French bread.

5 Uncover the casserole, arrange the bread slices overlapping on top and bake for a further 10–12 minutes, until golden and crisp.

COOK'S TIP

Add a crushed garlic clove to the parsley butter for extra flavour.

VARIATION

For a more Italian-tasting dish, replace the garlic and parsley bread topping with Pesto Toasts.

Country Chicken Braise with Rosemary Dumplings

Root vegetables are always cheap and nutritious, and combined with chicken they make tasty and economical casseroles.

Serves 4

INGREDIENTS

4 chicken quarters
2 tbsp sunflower oil
2 medium leeks
250 g/9 oz/1 cup carrots, chopped
250 g/9 oz/2 cups parsnips, chopped
2 small turnips, chopped

600 ml/1 pint/2^1/$_2$ cups chicken stock
3 tbsp Worcestershire sauce
2 sprigs fresh rosemary
salt and pepper

DUMPLINGS:
200 g/7 oz/1^3/$_4$ cups self-raising
  flour
100 g/3^1/$_2$ oz shredded suet
1 tbsp chopped rosemary leaves
cold water, to mix

1 Remove the skin from the chicken if you prefer. Heat the oil in a large, flameproof casserole or heavy saucepan and fry the chicken until golden. Using a slotted spoon, remove the chicken from the pan. Drain off the excess fat.

2 Trim and slice the leeks. Add the carrots, parsnips and turnips to the casserole and cook for 5 minutes, until lightly coloured. Return the chicken to the pan.

3 Add the chicken stock, Worcestershire sauce, rosemary and seasoning, then bring to the boil.

4 Reduce the heat, cover and simmer gently for about 50 minutes or until the juices run clear when the chicken is pierced with a skewer.

5 To make the dumplings, combine the flour, suet and rosemary leaves with salt and pepper in a bowl. Stir in just enough cold water to bind to a firm dough.

6 Form into 8 small balls and place on top of the chicken and vegetables. Cover and simmer for a further 10–12 minutes, until the dumplings are well risen. Serve with the casserole.

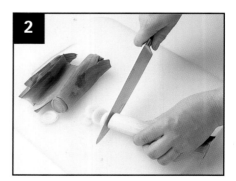

Chicken with Shallots in Wild Mushroom & Ginger Sauce

This recipe has an oriental flavour, which can be further enhanced with chopped spring onions (scallions), cinnamon and lemon grass.

Serves 6–8

INGREDIENTS

6 tbsp sesame oil
900 g/1³/₄ lb chicken meat
60 g/2 oz/¹/₂ cup flour, seasoned
32 shallots, sliced
500 g/1 lb 2 oz/6 cups wild
　mushrooms, roughly chopped

300 ml/¹/₂ pint/1¹/₄ cups chicken
　stock
2 tbsp Worcestershire sauce
1 tbsp honey
2 tbsp grated fresh root ginger
150 ml/¹/₄ pint/²/₃ cup yogurt

salt and pepper
flat leaf parsley, to garnish
wild rice and white rice, to serve

1 Heat the oil in a large frying pan (skillet). Coat the chicken in the seasoned flour and cook for about 4 minutes, until browned all over. Transfer to a large deep casserole and keep warm until required.

2 Slowly fry the shallots and mushrooms in the juices.

3 Add the chicken stock, Worcestershire sauce, honey and fresh ginger, then season to taste with salt and pepper.

4 Pour the mixture over the chicken, and cover the casserole with a lid or cooking foil.

5 Cook in the centre of a preheated oven, 150°C/300°F/ Gas Mark 2, for about 1½ hours, until the meat is very tender. Add the yogurt and cook for a further 10 minutes. Serve the casserole with a mixture of wild rice and white rice, and garnish with fresh parsley.

COOK'S TIP

Mushrooms can be stored in the refrigerator for 24–36 hours. Keep them in paper bags as they 'sweat' in plastic. You do not need to peel mushrooms but wild mushrooms must be washed thoroughly.

Garlic Chicken Casserole

This is a cassoulet with a twist – it is made with chicken instead of duck and lamb. Save time by using canned beans, such as borlotti or cannellini beans, which are both good in this dish.

Serves 4

INGREDIENTS

4 tbsp sunflower oil
900 g/1³/₄ lb chicken meat, chopped
250 g/9 oz/3 cups mushrooms, sliced
16 shallots
6 garlic cloves, crushed
1 tbsp plain (all-purpose) flour

250 ml/9 fl oz/1 cup white wine
250 ml/9 fl oz/1 cup chicken stock
1 bouquet garni (1 bay leaf, sprig
    thyme, celery, parsley & sage tied
    together with string)
400 g/14 oz can borlotti beans

salt and pepper
patty pans, to serve

1 Heat the sunflower oil in an ovenproof casserole and fry the chicken until browned all over. Remove the chicken from the casserole with a slotted spoon and set aside until required.

2 Add the mushrooms, shallots and garlic to the fat in the casserole and cook for 4 minutes.

3 Return the chicken to the casserole and sprinkle with the flour, then cook for a further 2 minutes.

4 Add the white wine and chicken stock, stir until boiling, then add the bouquet garni. Season well with salt and pepper.

5 Drain the borlotti beans and rinse thoroughly, then add to the casserole.

6 Cover and place in the centre of a preheated oven, 150°C/300°F/Gas Mark 2, for 2 hours. Remove the bouquet garni and serve the casserole with patty pans.

COOK'S TIP

Mushrooms are ideal in a low-fat diet because they are high in flavour and contain no fat. Experiment with the wealth of varieties that are now available from supermarkets.

COOK'S TIP

Serve the casserole with wholemeal (whole wheat) rice to make this filling dish go even further.

Old English Chicken Stewed in Ale

This is a slow-cooked, old-fashioned stew to warm up a wintery day. The rarebit toasts are a perfect accompaniment to soak up the rich juices, but if you prefer, serve the stew with jacket potatoes.

Serves 4–6

INGREDIENTS

4 large, skinless chicken thighs
2 tbsp plain (all-purpose) flour
2 tbsp English mustard powder
2 tbsp sunflower oil
15 g/^{1}/$_2$ oz/1 tbsp butter
4 small onions
600 ml/1 pint/2^1/$_2$ cups beer

2 tbsp Worcestershire sauce
3 tbsp chopped fresh sage leaves
salt and pepper

RAREBIT TOASTS:
60 g/2 oz/^{1}/$_2$ cup grated mature
   English Cheddar

1 tsp English mustard powder
1 tsp plain (all-purpose) flour
1 tsp Worcestershire sauce
1 tbsp beer
2 slices wholemeal (whole wheat)
   toast

1 Trim any excess fat from the chicken and toss in the flour and mustard powder to coat evenly. Heat the sunflower oil and butter in a large flameproof casserole and fry the chicken over a fairly high heat, turning occasionally, until golden. Remove the chicken from the casserole with a slotted spoon and keep hot.

2 Peel the onions and slice into wedges, then fry quickly until golden. Add the chicken, beer, Worcestershire sauce, fresh sage, and salt and pepper to taste. Bring to the boil, cover and simmer very gently for about 1½ hours, until the chicken is very tender.

3 Meanwhile, make the rarebit toasts: mix the cheese with the mustard powder, flour, Worcestershire sauce and beer. Spread the mixture over the toasts and cook under a hot grill (broiler) for about 1 minute, until melted and golden. Cut into triangles.

4 Stir the sage leaves into the chicken stew, bring to the boil and serve with the rarebit toasts, a green vegetable and new potatoes.

COOK'S TIP

If you do not have fresh sage, use 2 tsp of dried sage in step 2.

Rich Mediterranean Chicken Casserole

A colourful casserole packed with sunshine flavours from the Mediterranean.
Sun-dried tomatoes add a wonderful richness and you need very few to make this dish really special.

Serves 4

INGREDIENTS

8 chicken thighs
2 tbsp olive oil
1 medium red onion, sliced
2 garlic cloves, crushed
1 large red (bell) pepper, sliced thickly
thinly pared rind and juice
   of 1 small orange
125 ml/4 floz/$^{1}/_{2}$ cup chicken stock

400 g/14 oz can chopped tomatoes
25 g/1 oz/$^{1}/_{2}$ cup sun-dried
   tomatoes, thinly sliced
1 tbsp chopped fresh thyme
50 g/1$^{3}/_{4}$ oz/$^{1}/_{2}$ cup pitted black
   olives

salt and pepper
thyme sprigs and orange
   rind, to garnish
crusty fresh bread, to serve

1 In a heavy or non-stick large frying pan (skillet), fry the chicken without fat over a fairly high heat, turning occasionally until golden brown. Using a slotted spoon, drain off any excess fat from the chicken and transfer to a flameproof casserole.

2 Fry the onion, garlic and (bell) pepper in the pan over a moderate heat for 3–4 minutes. Transfer to the casserole.

3 Add the orange rind and juice, chicken stock, canned tomatoes and sun-dried tomatoes and stir to combine.

4 Bring to the boil then cover the casserole with a lid and simmer very gently over a low heat for about 1 hour, stirring occasionally. Add the chopped fresh thyme and pitted black olives, then adjust the seasoning with salt and pepper.

5 Scatter orange rind and thyme over the casserole to garnish, and serve with crusty bread.

COOK'S TIP

Sun-dried tomatoes have a dense texture and concentrated taste, and add intense flavour to slow-cooking casseroles.

Springtime Chicken Cobbler

Fresh spring vegetables are the basis of this colourful casserole, which is topped with hearty wholemeal (whole wheat) dumplings for a complete, healthy family meal.

Serves 4

INGREDIENTS

8 skinless chicken drumsticks
1 tbsp oil
1 small onion, sliced
350 g/12 oz/1¹/₂ cups baby carrots
2 baby turnips
125 g/4¹/₂ oz/1 cup broad (fava) beans or peas
1 tsp cornflour (cornstarch)

300 ml/¹/₂ pint/1¹/₄ cups chicken stock
2 bay leaves
salt and pepper

COBBLER TOPPING:
250 g/9 oz/2 cups wholemeal (whole wheat) plain (all-purpose) flour

2 tsp baking powder
25 g/1 oz/2 tbsp sunflower soft margarine
2 tsp dry wholegrain mustard
60 g/2 oz/¹/₂ cup Cheddar cheese, grated
skimmed milk, to mix
sesame seeds, to sprinkle

1 Fry the chicken in the oil, turning, until golden brown. Drain well and place in an ovenproof casserole. Sauté the onion for 2–3 minutes to soften.

2 Wash and trim the carrots and turnips and cut into equal-sized pieces. Add to the casserole with the onions and beans or peas.

3 Blend the cornflour (cornstarch) with a little of the stock, then stir in the rest and heat gently, stirring until boiling. Pour into the casserole and add the bay leaves, salt and pepper.

4 Cover tightly and bake in a preheated oven, 200°C/400°F/ Gas Mark 6, for 50–60 minutes, or until the chicken juices run clear when pierced with a skewer.

5 For the topping, sift the flour and baking powder. Mix in the margarine with a fork. Stir in the mustard, the cheese and enough milk to form a fairly soft dough.

6 Roll out and cut 16 rounds with a 4 cm/1½ inch cutter. Uncover the casserole, arrange the scone (biscuit) rounds on top, then brush with milk and sprinkle with sesame seeds. Bake in the oven for 20 minutes or until the topping is golden and firm.

Roast Chicken with Coriander (Cilantro) & Garlic

This recipe for chicken is coated with a fresh-flavoured marinade then roasted.
Try serving it with rice, yogurt and salad.

Serves 4-6

INGREDIENTS

3 sprigs fresh coriander (cilantro), chopped
4 garlic cloves
$\frac{1}{2}$ tsp salt

1 tsp pepper
4 tbsp lemon juice
4 tbsp olive oil
1 large chicken

pepper
sprig of fresh parsley, to garnish
boiled potatoes and carrots, to serve

1 Place the chopped coriander (cilantro), garlic, salt, pepper, lemon juice and olive oil in a pestle and mortar and pound together or blend in a food processor. Chill for 4 hours to allow the flavours to develop.

2 Place the chicken in a roasting tin (pan). Coat generously with the coriander (cilantro) and garlic mixture.

3 Sprinkle with pepper and roast in a preheated oven, 190°C/375°F/Gas Mark 5, on a low shelf for 1½ hours, basting every 20 minutes with the coriander (cilantro) mixture. If the chicken starts to turn brown, cover with foil. Garnish with parsley and serve with the potatoes and carrots.

COOK'S TIP

For pounding small quantities it is best to use a pestle and mortar so as little as possible of the mixture is left in the container.

VARIATION

Any fresh herb can be used in this recipe instead of the coriander (cilantro). Tarragon or thyme are a good combination with chicken.

Roast Chicken Breasts with Bacon & Dripping(s) Triangles

Chicken suprêmes have a little bit of the wing bone remaining which makes them easy to pick up and eat. In this recipe, a tart, fruity sauce perfectly complements the chicken and dripping(s) triangles.

Serves 8

INGREDIENTS

60 g/2 oz/4 tbsp butter
juice of 1 lemon
250 g/9 oz/1 cup redcurrants or
   cranberries

1–2 tbsp muscovado sugar
8 chicken suprêmes or breasts
16 slices of streaky bacon
thyme

60 g/2 oz/4 tbsp beef dripping(s)
4 slices of bread, cut into triangles
salt and pepper

1 Heat the butter in a saucepan, add the lemon juice, redcurrants or cranberries, muscovado sugar and salt and pepper to taste. Cook for 1 minute and allow to cool until required.

2 Meanwhile, season the chicken with salt and pepper. Wrap 2 slices of streaky bacon around each breast and sprinkle with thyme.

3 Wrap each breast in a piece of lightly greased foil and place in a roasting tin (pan). Roast in a preheated oven, 200°C/400°F/Gas Mark 6, for 15 minutes. Remove the foil and roast for another 10 minutes.

4 Heat the dripping(s) in a frying pan (skillet), add the bread triangles and fry on both sides until golden brown.

5 Arrange the triangles on a large serving plate and top each with a chicken breast. Serve with a spoonful of the fruit sauce.

COOK'S TIP

You can use either chopped fresh thyme or dried thyme in this recipe, but remember that dried herbs have a stronger flavour so you only need half the quantity compared to fresh herbs.

Mediterranean-style Sunday Roast

A roast that is full of Mediterranean flavour. A mixture of feta cheese, rosemary and sun-dried tomatoes is stuffed under the chicken skin, then roasted with garlic, new potatoes and vegetables.

Serves 6

INGREDIENTS

2.5 kg/5 lb 8 oz chicken
sprigs of fresh rosemary
175 g/6 oz/³/4 cup feta cheese,
  coarsely grated
2 tbsp sun-dried tomato paste
60 g/2 oz/4 tbsp butter, softened

1 bulb garlic
1 kg/2 lb 4 oz new potatoes, halved
  if large
1 each red, green and yellow
  (bell) pepper, cut into chunks
3 courgettes (zucchini), sliced thinly

2 tbsp olive oil
2 tbsp plain (all-purpose) flour
600 ml/1 pint/2¹/2 cups chicken stock
salt and pepper

1 Rinse the chicken inside and out with cold water and drain well. Carefully cut between the skin and the top of the breast meat using a small pointed knife. Slide a finger into the slit and carefully enlarge it to form a pocket. Continue until the skin is completely lifted away from both breasts and the top of the legs.

2 Chop the leaves from 3 rosemary stems. Mix with the feta, sun-dried tomato paste, butter and pepper then spoon under the skin. Put the chicken in a large roasting tin (pan), cover with foil and cook in a preheated oven, 190°C/375°F/Gas Mark 5, for 20 minutes per 500 g/1 lb 2 oz plus 20 minutes.

3 Break the garlic bulb into cloves but do not peel. Add the vegetables to the chicken after 40 minutes.

4 Drizzle with oil, tuck in a few stems of rosemary and season well. Cook for the remaining time, removing the foil for the last 40 minutes to brown the chicken.

5 Transfer the chicken to a serving platter. Place some of the vegetables around the chicken and transfer the remainder to a warmed serving dish. Pour the fat out of the roasting tin (pan) and stir the flour into the remaining pan juices. Cook for 2 minutes then gradually stir in the stock. Bring to the boil, stirring until thickened. Strain into a sauce boat and serve with the chicken.

Gardener's Chicken

Any combination of small, young vegetables can be roasted with the chicken,
such as courgettes (zucchini), leeks and onions.

Serves 4

INGREDIENTS

250 g/9 oz/4 cups parsnips,
  peeled and chopped
125 g/4^1/$_2$ oz/^{3}/$_4$ cup carrots, peeled
  and chopped
25 g/1 oz/^{1}/$_2$ cup fresh breadcrumbs
^{1}/$_4$ tsp grated nutmeg

1 tbsp chopped fresh parsley
1.5 kg/3 lb 5 oz chicken
bunch of parsley
^{1}/$_2$ onion
25 g/1 oz/2 tbsp butter, softened
4 tbsp olive oil

500 g/1 lb 2 oz new potatoes,
  scrubbed
500 g/1 lb 2 oz baby carrots
  washed and trimmed
salt and pepper
chopped fresh parsley, to garnish

1 To make the stuffing, put the parsnips and carrots into a pan, half cover with water and bring to the boil. Cover the pan and simmer until tender. Drain well then purée in a blender or food processor. Transfer the purée to a bowl and leave to cool.

2 Mix in the breadcrumbs, nutmeg and parsley and season with salt and pepper.

3 Put the stuffing into the neck end of the chicken and push a little under the skin over the breast meat. Secure the flap of skin with a small metal skewer or cocktail stick.

4 Place the bunch of parsley and onion inside the cavity of the chicken, then place the chicken in a large roasting tin (pan).

5 Spread the butter over the skin and season with salt and pepper, cover with foil and place in a preheated oven, 190°C/375°F/Gas Mark 5, for 30 minutes.

6 Meanwhile, heat the oil in a frying pan (skillet), and lightly brown the potatoes.

7 Transfer the potatoes to the roasting tin (pan) and add the baby carrots. Baste the chicken and continue to cook for a further hour, basting the chicken and vegetables after 30 minutes. Remove the foil for the last 20 minutes to allow the skin to crisp. Garnish the vegetables with chopped parsley and serve.

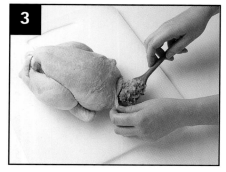

Chicken Cajun-Style

These spicy chicken wings are good served with a chilli salsa and salad. Alternatively, if this is too spicy for your taste, try a sour cream and chive dip.

Serves 4

INGREDIENTS

16 chicken wings
4 tsp paprika
2 tsp ground coriander
1 tsp celery salt
1 tsp ground cumin
$1/2$ tsp cayenne pepper

$1/2$ tsp salt
1 tbsp oil
2 tbsp red wine vinegar
fresh parsley, to garnish
cherry tomatoes and mixed salad
   leaves, to serve

1 Wash the chicken wings and pat dry with absorbent paper towels. Remove the wing tips with kitchen scissors.

2 Mix together the paprika, coriander, celery salt, cumin, cayenne pepper, salt, oil and red wine vinegar.

3 Rub this mixture over the wings to coat evenly and set aside, in the refrigerator, for at least 1 hour to allow the flavours to permeate the chicken.

4 Cook the chicken wings on a preheated barbecue (grill), occasionally brushing with oil, for about 15 minutes, turning often until cooked through. Garnish with fresh parsley and serve with cherry tomatoes, mixed salad leaves and a sauce of your choice.

COOK'S TIP

To save time, you can buy ready-made Cajun spice seasoning to rub over the chicken wings.

VARIATION

Although chicken wings do not have much meat on them, they are small and easy to pick up with your fingers which makes them ideal for barbecues (grills). However, they can also be enjoyed fried or roasted.

Sweet & Sour Drumsticks

Chicken drumsticks are marinated to impart a tangy, sweet and sour flavour and a shiny glaze.

Serves 4

INGREDIENTS

8 chicken drumsticks
4 tbsp red wine vinegar
2 tbsp tomato purée (paste)
2 tbsp soy sauce

2 tbsp clear honey
1 tbsp Worcestershire sauce
1 garlic clove
good pinch cayenne pepper

salt and pepper
sprig of fresh parsley, to garnish

1 Skin the chicken, if desired, and slash 2–3 times with a sharp knife.

2 Lay the chicken drumsticks side by side in a shallow non-metallic container.

3 Mix the red wine vinegar, tomato purée (paste), soy sauce, honey, Worcestershire sauce, garlic and cayenne pepper together and pour over the chicken drumsticks.

4 Leave to marinate in the refrigerator for 1 hour. Cook the drumsticks on a preheated barbecue (grill) for about 20 minutes, brushing with the marinade and turning during cooking. Garnish with parsley and serve with a crisp salad.

COOK'S TIP

For a tangy flavour, add the juice of 1 lime to the marinade. While the drumsticks are grilling (broiling), check regularly to ensure that they are not burning.

VARIATION

This sweet and sour marinade would also work well with pork or prawns (shrimp). Thread pork cubes or prawns (shrimp) on to skewers with (bell) peppers and button onions.

Spicy Chicken Tortillas

Serve these easy-to-prepare tortillas to friends or as a special family supper.
The chicken filling has a mild, mellow spicy heat and a fresh salad makes a perfect accompaniment.

Serves 4

INGREDIENTS

2 tbsp oil
8 skinless, boneless chicken
  thighs, sliced
1 onion, chopped
2 garlic cloves, chopped
1 tsp cumin seeds, roughly crushed
2 large dried chillies, sliced

400 g/14 oz can tomatoes
400 g/14 oz can red kidney
  beans, drained
150 ml/^{1}/$_4$ pint/^{2}/$_3$ cup chicken stock
2 tsp sugar
salt and pepper
lime wedges, to garnish

TO SERVE:
1 large ripe avocado
1 lime
8 soft tortillas
250 ml/9 fl oz/1 cup thick yogurt

1 Heat the oil in a large frying pan (skillet) or wok, add the chicken and fry for 3 minutes until golden. Add the onion and fry for 5 minutes, stirring until browned. Add the garlic, cumin and chillies, with their seeds, and cook for about 1 minute.

2 Add the tomatoes, kidney beans, stock, sugar and salt and pepper to taste. Bring to the boil, breaking up the tomatoes. Cover and simmer for 15 minutes.

Remove the lid and cook for 5 minutes, stirring occasionally until the sauce has thickened.

3 Halve the avocado, discard the stone and scoop out the flesh on to a plate. Mash the avocado with a fork. Cut half of the lime into 8 thin wedges. Squeeze the juice from the remaining lime over the avocado.

4 Warm the tortillas following the instructions on the packet.

Put two tortillas on each serving plate, fill with the chicken mixture and top with spoonfuls of avocado and yogurt. Garnish the tortillas with lime wedges.

VARIATION

For a vegetarian filling, replace the chicken with 400 g/14 oz canned pinto or cannellini beans and use vegetable stock instead of the chicken stock.

This is a Parragon Book
First published in 2003

Parragon
Queen Street House
4 Queen Street, Bath, BA1 1HE, UK

Copyright © Parragon 2003

All recipes and photography compiled from material
created by 'Haldane Mason', and 'The Foundry'.

Cover design by Shelley Doyle.

ISBN: 1-40540-820-0

Printed in China

NOTE

This book uses imperial and metric measurements. Follow the same units
of measurement throughout; do not mix imperial and metric. All spoon
measurements are level; teaspoons are assumed to be 5 ml and
tablespoons are assumed to be 15 ml. Unless otherwise stated, milk is
assumed to be whole milk, eggs and individual vegetables such as
potatoes are medium, and pepper is freshly ground black pepper.

The times given for each recipe are an approximate guide only because
the preparation times may differ according to the techniques used by
different people and the cooking times may vary as a result of the type of
oven used.

Recipes using raw or very lightly cooked eggs should be avoided by
infants, the elderly, pregnant women, convalescents and anyone suffering
from an illness.